CORPORATE AMERICA
Google
Joy Gregory
Google
LIGHTBOX
openlightbox.com

Lightbox is an all-inclusive digital solution for the teaching and learning of curriculum topics in an original, groundbreaking way. Lightbox is based on National Curriculum Standards.

STANDARD FEATURES OF LIGHTBOX

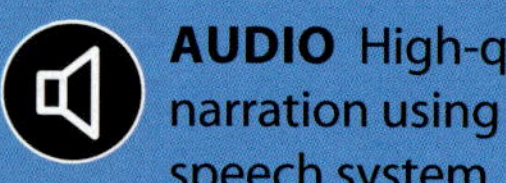

AUDIO High-quality narration using text-to-speech system

ACTIVITIES Printable PDFs that can be emailed and graded

SLIDESHOWS Pictorial overviews of key concepts

VIDEOS Embedded high-definition video clips

WEBLINKS Curated links to external, child-safe resources

TRANSPARENCIES Step-by-step layering of maps, diagrams, charts, and timelines

INTERACTIVE MAPS Interactive maps and aerial satellite imagery

QUIZZES Ten multiple choice questions that are automatically graded and emailed for teacher assessment

KEY WORDS Matching key concepts to their definitions

Contents

Introduction

Google is the name of the world's most popular internet search engine. It is also the name of the search engine's creator, a multinational technology company based in the United States. Formed in the late 1990s, Google owns a number of technology-based services, including Google Maps, YouTube, Android, Google Play, and Google Cloud. Google also makes computer **hardware** for mobile phones, laptops, and **digital streaming** devices.

In 2015, Google became part of a new company called Alphabet Inc. With Google as its largest business unit, Alphabet is one of the most **profitable conglomerates** in the world. Alphabet's other businesses include a **venture capital** business and a health technology company.

Every second, Google handles approximately **40,000 search queries.**

Google's search page is available in more than **150 languages.**

By 2017, Google accounted for **$89.5 billion** of Alphabet's **$90.3 billion** in sales.

Google delivers search results in **1/8 of a second.**

Sundar Pichai was named Google's chief executive officer (CEO) in 2015, after rising through the company ranks. As CEO, Pichai is responsible for ensuring Google continues on a successful track.

Founding Date	Became Public	Opening Price	Stock Symbol
1998	August 2004	$85.00 USD	nasdaq: GOOGL

Beginnings

Google was founded in 1998 by Larry Page and Sergey Brin, two computer science students at Stanford University. In 1996, Brin and Page began working on a research project together. A mutual interest in developing tools for the World Wide Web led them to build BackRub, a search engine that used "back links" to rank information stored on the Web. By the time the search engine had mapped the entire Web, BackRub had been renamed Google.

Word of the search engine began to spread, first throughout the academic community and then into business circles. In August 1998, Brin and Page received a check for $100,000 from their first **investor**, Andy Bechtolsheim. Bechtolsheim was the co-founder of Sun Microsystems, a tech company located in California's Silicon Valley. More investors soon followed, bringing in another $900,000. Brin and Page used the money to establish their company. They moved the business from their dorm rooms at Stanford into their first office, located in a friend's garage.

Within two years of Google's launch, the search engine was being used for millions of searches every day. Google soon expanded, adding news, mapping, and email services before branching into hardware devices. As more staff came on board to handle the demands of the growing company, it became necessary to find larger office space. After a few moves, the company finally settled in a building in Mountain View, California, in 2004. The building is now known as the Googleplex.

The garage that served as Google's first office belonged to Susan Wojcicki, now CEO of YouTube.

The company continued to grow, developing new products under the Google banner and expanding into other ventures. By 2015, Google was so diverse that a **parent company**, Alphabet, was set up. Alphabet runs both Google and Other Bets, an umbrella for Google's side businesses.

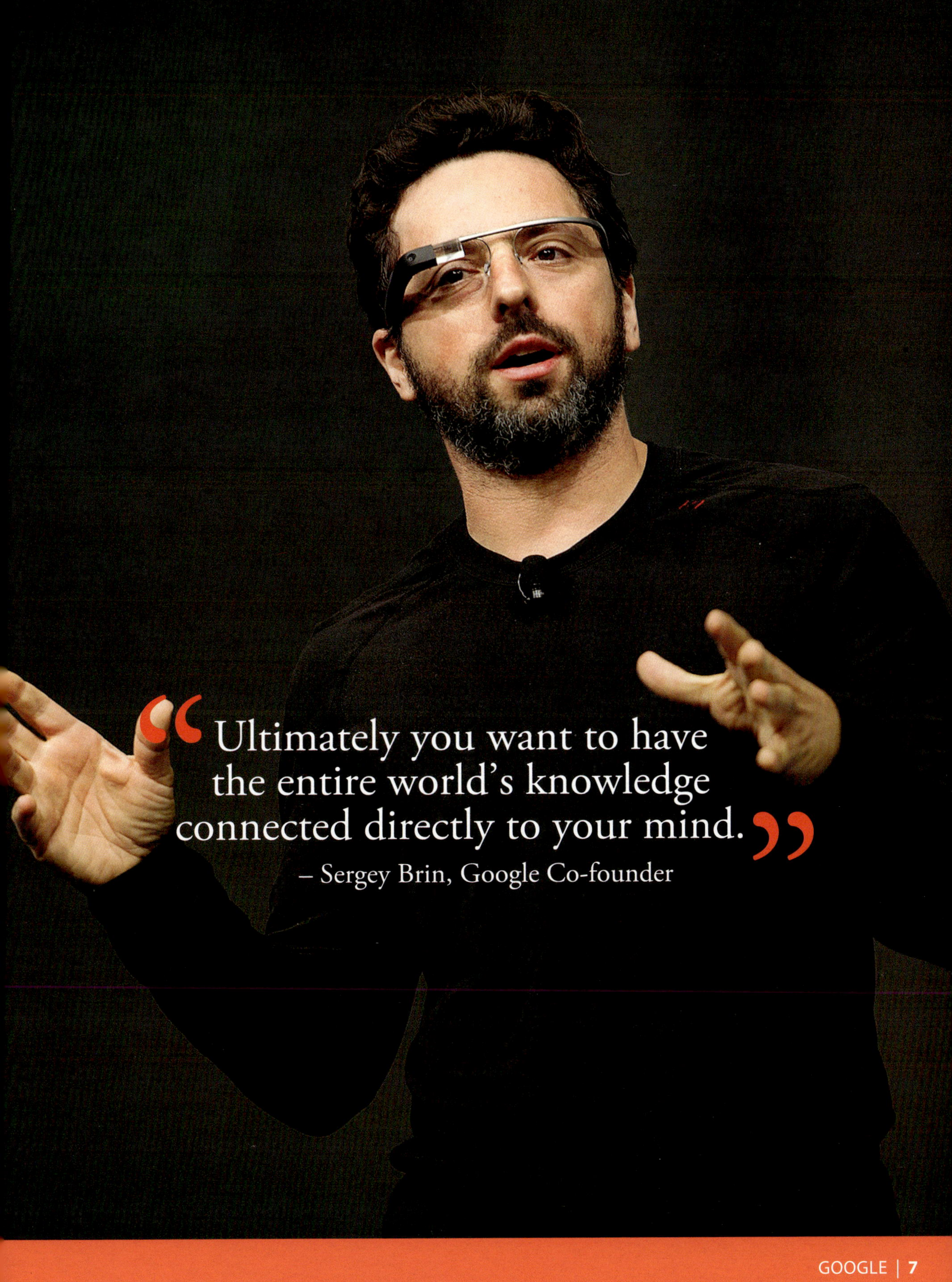
"Ultimately you want to have the entire world's knowledge connected directly to your mind."
– Sergey Brin, Google Co-founder

Corporate Timeline

From its humble beginnings in a university dorm to its current status as one of the world's most successful companies, Google's history is one of rapid expansion. Google has **diversified** through internal growth and corporate **acquisitions**. Today, the company sells products unheard of before 1998.

1998

A Company Is Born
Larry Page and Sergey Brin sign the papers to **incorporate** Google.

1998

The Google Garage
Google opens its first office in a garage in Menlo Park, California.

2002

Google News Begins
Google launches a news service that scans thousands of news articles and then delivers the top U.S. and world news stories to Google News users.

2004

The Googleplex Opens
Google opens the Googleplex, its new office in Mountain View, California.

2005

Google Geography
The company launches Google Maps and Google Earth, making it easy for users to search neighborhoods all over the world.

Chrome Speeds the Search
Google releases Chrome, a free web browser designed to be a fast, secure, and easy-to-use way of browsing the internet.

2008

Alphabet Inc.
Alphabet Inc. is created as the parent company of Google.

2015

2006

2007

A New Verb
The Oxford English Dictionary adds a new verb, "google," meaning the act of searching for information on the internet.

Gmail Launch
Google offers a no-fee email service called Gmail.

Google Today

Now used about 3.5 billion times every day, Google Search is capable of finding any piece of information stored on the World Wide Web. By 2017, Google accounted for close to 80 percent of all internet searches. Other Google innovations have transformed how people live, work, and play.

Google owes much of its success to its commitment to imagining, and then creating, new ways to connect users with information. By **digitizing** information stored in traditional archives, Google is preserving historical data and making it accessible to all internet users. With Google Maps and Google Earth, the company has literally mapped the planet. Over time, Google has also added other internet services. Gmail is the company's email service, while Google+ is a networking site. People can store their photographs using Google Photos, and play games and music with Google Play. Google also offers Google Cloud, an internet-based business service for document storage, data analysis, and data sharing. By 2016, Google's Android mobile phone technology powered close to 88 percent of the global smartphone market.

Google's commitment to technological innovation is what led to the creation of its parent company. This move allowed Google to develop ideas in areas outside the Google **brand**. Alphabet oversees Google's continued growth in web-based technology and tech innovations. The Other Bets division connects internet users through fiber optics technology and builds technology to run homes and offices. It also provides start-up money for companies in the fields of life sciences, health care, artificial intelligence (AI), robotics, and cybersecurity. As a result of this expansion, Alphabet has now become the second-most valuable company in the world.

One of the companies run under Alphabet's Other Bets division is Nest Labs. Nest specializes in home automation, developing internet-connected home hardware such as security and safety devices.

> "Basically, our goal is to organize the world's information and to make it universally accessible and useful."
>
> – Larry Page,
> Google Co-founder
> and Alphabet CEO

A World of Google

Google has more than 70 offices in 50 countries around the world. Besides being one of the world's best-known companies, Google also ranks high on the list of best places to work. Google offices are designed to encourage employees to be creative thinkers.

1 **Corporate Headquarters** Google's international headquarters is located in Mountain View, California. The site, with its bike paths and sculpture gardens, is a popular tourist attraction.

2 **Venice Beach Office** A giant pair of binoculars frames the entrance to the Google office in Venice Beach, California. Inside, workers have access to a pool table and vintage arcade games.

3 **Toronto Office** Each of the floors in Google's office in Toronto, Canada, is color-coded to reflect the colors in the Google **logo**. Employees at this office can play miniature golf on the office roof.

4 **Zurich Office** Private work pods give Google employees at the Zurich, Switzerland, office a quiet place to work or hold small meetings. To add a little fun to the day, the office also includes a firepole, a slide, and foam-filled bathtubs for staff to use while meditating.

5 **Sydney Office** The Google office in Sydney, Australia, includes a variety of work-play options. The choices run from video games to table tennis, chess, billiards, and musical instruments.

Branding Google

Google's founders created a successful business based on a technology few people used, understood, or even thought they needed. That first Google product, and the ones that followed, turned computer users into internet users by giving them reliable and easy-to-use technology. Twenty years later, Google is one of the most recognized brands in the world.

Free for All When Page and Brin founded Google, their goal was to organize as much information as possible and make it accessible to people all over the world. Their initial steps toward this goal far surpassed anything else that had been created at the time. The company has maintained a leadership position in the tech industry ever since. While most other search engines also offer their services free of charge, Google has been able to amass more information and organize it more effectively. The intuitive nature of Google's search engine allows it to provide users with the information they need in an efficient and structured manner. People have come to trust Google to understand how they think. This trust has encouraged their loyalty. When Google develops new products, it has an established customer base ready to use them.

Creative Thinkers Google has built a reputation on being a company that thinks creatively and strives for innovation. The company's continued success depends on creating next-generation technology. Google encourages its employees to "think big but start small." Google Books, for example, could not have digitized and archived more than 10 million documents without beginning with a single page. Google also advises its workers to learn as they go, and to apply that knowledge to making new and better products. That willingness to try new ideas includes an openness to learning from failure. Google keeps ideas that work, and it changes or drops ideas that do not.

A Collaborative Approach

Google brands itself as a company that believes in building community. It values the input of others and has put systems in place to encourage feedback. Most of the code written for computers began as open source **software**. This framework allows computer programmers to contribute lines of computer code that others can use, improve, and share at no cost. Unlike companies that legally protect all of their code, Google views open source software as a way to encourage coders to work together to solve problems. Over time, Google has released more than 20 million lines of open source code. The company's commitment to supporting open source platforms was key to its launching of the new Google Open Source website in 2017. This site provides information about how Google uses, releases, and supports open source software.

Google

Company Name

The name "Google" is a misspelling of the world "googol," which means an unfathomable number. Page and Brin named their search engine Google to indicate its infinite reach. The company name is based on the name of the search engine.

Company Logo

The Google logo features a capital "G" followed by lowercase letters. The letters are vivid shades of blue, red, yellow, and green. The goal of the logo is to present the company as friendly and approachable.

Company Slogan

Google's **slogan**, "Don't Be Evil," was adopted shortly after the company was founded. It is also part of Google's employee code of conduct.

The Art of Selling

Google understands the importance of keeping its name at the forefront of people's minds. For this reason, it has used a variety of marketing techniques designed to showcase the company's products, its creativity, and its connection with its users. The company knows that attracting more users to its products will also attract advertisers. It is through advertising that companies like Google earn most of their money.

Call It Google Google reinforces its market dominance in the minds of users and investors by including the word "Google" in the names of most of its tech tools, such as Google Chrome, Google Play, and Google Maps. Some of Google's acquisitions break with this branding strategy, however. These include YouTube, a video sharing platform, Picasa, a photo sharing platform, and Blogger, a blogging platform. Here, market data showed that users identified more with the original names, so Google did not rebrand the companies.

Google Doodles Google's logo has been criticized for its lack of style, but this simplistic logo has generated a great deal of attention. Some versions have even attracted news media coverage and widespread internet shares. The first Google Doodle was made in 1998 when the company's founders added a stick figure to the second "o" in Google on an office memo. It was a tribute to the Burning Man Festival Larry Page and Sergey Brin had attended. In 2000, the company started to remix the plain logo more regularly, often to celebrate historical figures, holidays, and special events such as the solar eclipse of 2017.

Year in Search At the end of every year, Google releases a video that provides an overview of the top Google searches for the past year. Video and audio clips are played, reminding viewers of events that occurred over the course of the year. As the images are shown, key words appear in a Google search box placed in the middle of the screen. These words link the images to themes of the year. The video aims to show how Google plays an integral role in transmitting information to people and how it is an intrinsic part of the global community.

More than **2,000** **Google Doodles** have been created since the year 2000.

Every day, almost **5 billion videos** are watched on **YouTube**.

More than **85%** of Google's earnings **come from advertising**.

Competitors

Amazon and Apple are two of Google's main competitors. All three companies compete in the areas of internet services, computer software, and consumer electronics. Google also competes with internet corporations such as Facebook. Like Google, Facebook makes most of its money from advertisers that pay to have their ads shown on its pages.

amazon

STOCK SYMBOL nasdaq: AMZN

Amazon.com is the world's largest online retailer. Founded in 1994, the company sells and ships merchandise to consumers and businesses around the world. Amazon competes with Google for online shoppers. Like Google, Amazon also makes and sells electronic gadgets and sells internet-based business services. Every buyer that goes directly to Amazon.com without searching Google first costs Google advertising **revenue**.

STOCK SYMBOL nasdaq: AAPL

Established in 1976, Apple Inc. designs, manufactures, and sells a variety of digital devices. It is responsible for many of the world's most recent technological innovations, including the iPad and iPhone. Like Google, Apple has also developed a computer operating system for desktop computers, tablets, and mobile phones. Both Google and Apple regularly release new **apps**, including games, for their products.

facebook

STOCK SYMBOL nasdaq: FB

Facebook, Inc. started in 2004 as an internet-based social network. Today, people, organizations, and companies use Facebook to communicate with others. Google and Facebook offer similar services, including a news service, messaging tool, and mobile apps. Popular mobile apps owned by Facebook include Instagram and Whatsapp.

Comparison Chart

Businesses keep records to track their **assets**, **liabilities**, profits, and losses. Companies use this data to guide expansion and cost-cutting decisions. Investors use the information to help them decide where to invest their money. They will also refer to a company's **market capitalization** to gauge public confidence in the business.

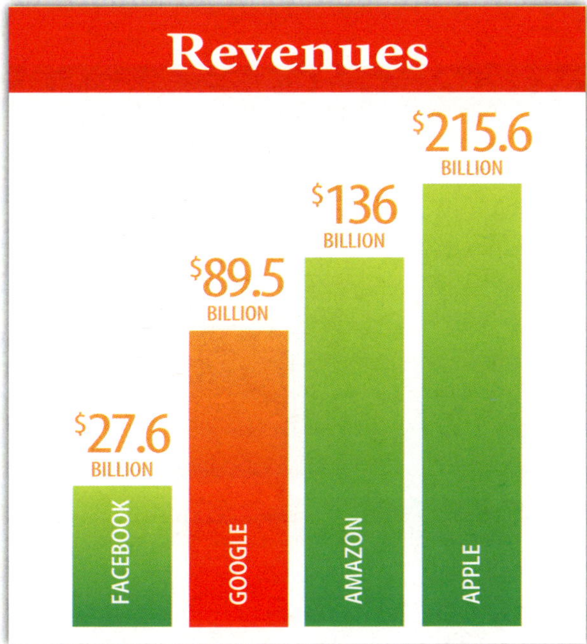

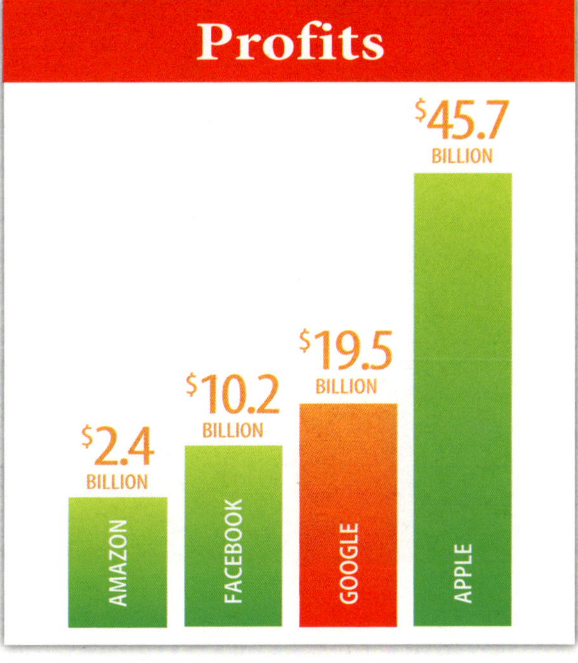

2016 Figures

Innovation and Technology

Google Home

"Okay, Google." This is what users say to start Google Home, a voice-activated speaker powered by Google Assistant. Launched in 2016, Google Home can make phone calls and answer questions about traffic, weather, sports, and finance. It also plays music, podcasts, or radio, and connects to devices in a person's home, including lights and thermostats.

Google Glass

First released in 2012, Google Glass, a head-mounted device resembling glasses, never found a market with consumers. Most people were not interested in using glasses to access the internet. However, by 2017, the technology was earning praise from industrial users. Google Glass Enterprise Edition boosts workplace productivity and quality by letting users work with both hands while simultaneously reading data, such as instructions, from the glasses.

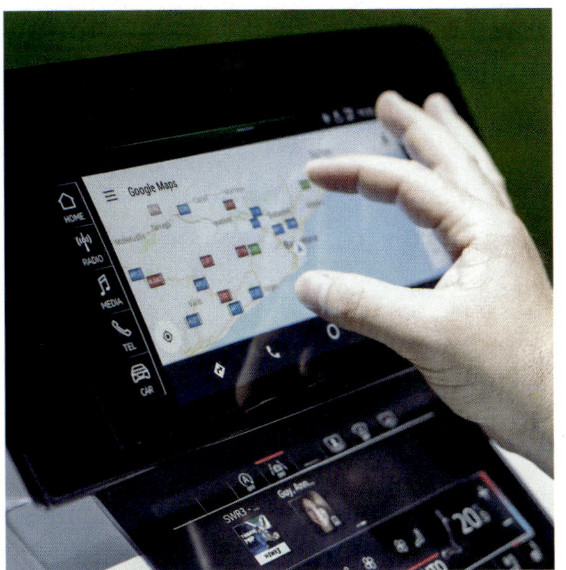

Google Maps

More than half of the world's smartphones are equipped with Google Maps, an internet-based mapping service that provides aerial and street-level views of most of the world's roads. People use the tool to plan travel routes by foot, automobile, bicycle, or, where available, public transportation. Companies and organizations make it easy for their customers to find directions to their locations by embedding Google Maps into their websites.

Waymo

Initiated in 2009 as the Google self-driving car project, the company Waymo was started in 2016. Operated under Alphabet, Waymo aims to put a fully **autonomous** car on the U.S. automobile market. The vehicle will take passengers from one place to another without ever requiring them to take control of the wheel. By 2017, Waymo was logging 25,000 autonomous miles (40,200 kilometers) a week, mostly driven on city streets. Waymo launched its first public trial in Phoenix, Arizona, that same year.

Giving Back

Corporate **philanthropy** allows organizations to give back to their communities while linking the company brand with the causes that matter to those communities. In 2005, Google formed Google.org. This organization connects Google to **non-profit organizations** working in four key areas—education, economic opportunity, inclusion, and crisis response.

Story Weaver Since 2013, Google.org has invested $3.85 million in Pratham Books through an educational program called Story Weaver. This online platform creates free stories for children all over the world. Thanks to open source technology, the stories can be translated into more than 60 languages. Story Weaver makes it easy for literacy organizations, teachers, and parents to find, download, and even print stories that match a student's reading level and language preference.

Code for America In 2017, Google.org provided $1.5 million for a two-year project called Code for America. Code for America will develop new technologies to help millions of American job seekers find the resources they need to get new or better jobs. This fits with Google.org's commitment to helping people access opportunities that can help them break the cycle of poverty. Code for America is developing user-friendly tech tools to help job seekers access training and job search assistance. These include a technology called CareerPathNOLA, which helps job seekers prepare to visit a job center.

Equal Justice Initiative The Equal Justice Initiative (EJI) focuses on issues related to equality, or the idea that all people deserve to be treated as equals. Since 2016, Google.org has invested $2.4 million in two EJI programs. One is a museum that examines African American history and issues related to race, imprisonment, and police violence. The second is the Memorial to Peace and Justice, which commemorates victims of lynchings in the United States. The memorial is slated to open in 2018, in Montgomery, Alabama.

By 2019, Code for America will connect **30,000** U.S. job seekers with **training and job search support**.

Google has given **$11 million in resources**, including money and volunteer hours, to Khan Academy, an online tutorial school that provides high-quality, free education to all users.

The U.S. Center for Policing Equity received **$5 million** from Google.org to collect and analyze data about police behavior and race.

Into the Future

Two decades after it began, Google is still working hard to make it easy for people to access information on the internet. Looking ahead, there are signs that the popularity of Google Search will increase as internet searches become a more routine part of people's daily lives. Research indicates that the number of searches conducted on mobile devices, including tablets, mobile phones, and laptops, will also continue to rise.

Google products, including Android, Google Maps, YouTube, Google Play, and Gmail, already attract more than 1 billion users each per month. Google believes the next billion users will be attracted by computer applications that use AI and **machine learning**. AI will improve existing Google applications, such as Search and Cloud. It will also be used in new technology. This includes driverless cars, which are becoming more reliable as the tech industry continues to develop and improve these technologies.

Google will face key challenges in the years to come. The company must remain responsive to advertisers' concerns about certain content, especially hate speech that attacks people on the basis of gender or race, or content by terrorists who inspire acts of violence. Computer viruses and **malware** also present ongoing threats to business. More recently, Google has come under fire for concerns that it has a market **monopoly**. People feel that Google is so dominant that other companies cannot compete for business and skilled employees.

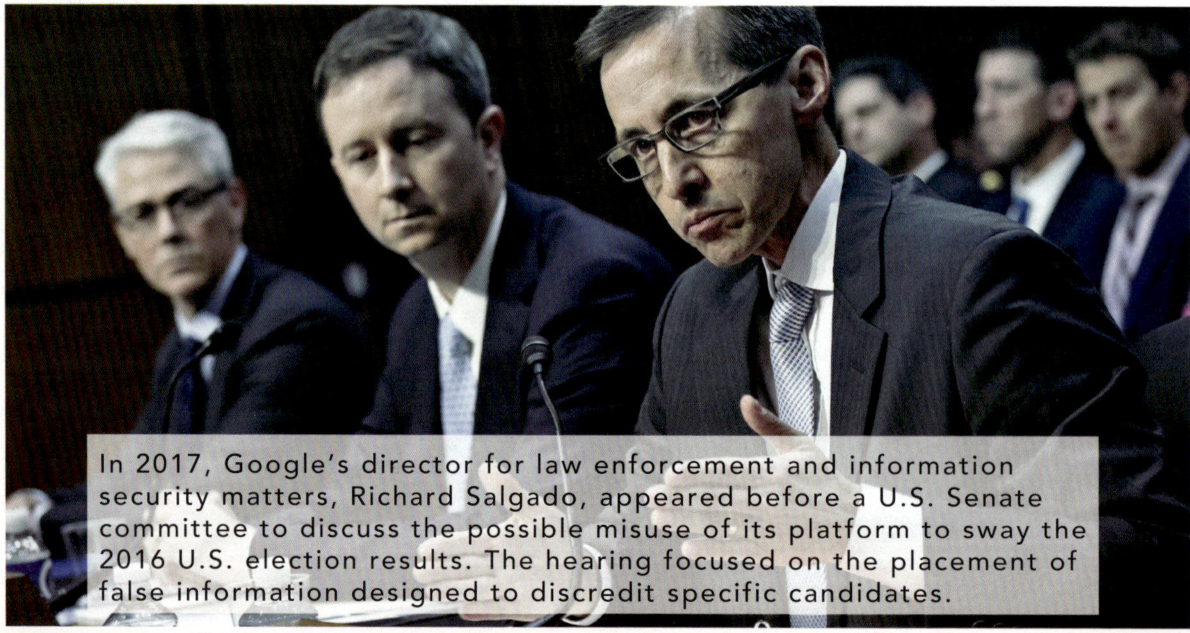

In 2017, Google's director for law enforcement and information security matters, Richard Salgado, appeared before a U.S. Senate committee to discuss the possible misuse of its platform to sway the 2016 U.S. election results. The hearing focused on the placement of false information designed to discredit specific candidates.

Google will continue to expand its product line into new areas and to enhance its existing products, much like it has with its Daydream View VR headset. Launched in 2016, the set, which allows users to play games and videos in a 360-degree environment, was updated after only one year on the market.

Careers at Google

Google and its parent company, Alphabet Inc., employ thousands of highly skilled people. Located in offices all over the world, these individuals work hard to design and deliver technology that millions of people rely on in their personal and business lives.

CEO

$200 million per year

The job of chief executive officer (CEO) is usually the highest position within a company. The CEO is responsible for creating and executing the company's long-term goals. He or she is in charge of all aspects of the business. A CEO helps the company run smoothly, guiding it in a successful direction. CEOs oversee many departments within the company, managing staff and delegating tasks. The CEO usually reports to a **board of directors**.

Internal Communications Manager

$100,000–$217,000 per year

Google's internal communications managers create print- and web-based materials to tell others about what the company is doing. These managers have strong written and verbal communication skills. They are good at communicating complicated issues to other employees and to the board of directors. Their campaigns help Google's external communicators, including its marketing team, produce material for investors, consumers, and journalists.

People Consultant

$65,000–$71,000 per year

People consultants work in Google's people operations department. They help employees understand work contracts and the benefits available to them. Google's people consultants know how to promote teamwork. They are good at organizing and coaching people who work together. They also help Google employees learn how to manage conflict.

Software Engineer

$124,000–$176,000 per year

Google's software engineers usually hold degrees in computer science. They work in several programming languages, and might specialize in areas such as web application development, open source systems, machine learning, or security software. To encourage finding new solutions to tech problems, Google lets its software engineers switch teams and projects as needed.

Activity

Google is always developing new products that help people use the internet more effectively. If you were to suggest a new product for Google, what would it be?

Imagine that Google has invited you to their headquarters to pitch, or promote, your product idea to them. Prepare a presentation using the following questions as a guide.

1. Who might be attending your presentation? How will knowing your audience affect how you approach your presentation?

2. What are your product's key selling points? How do they fit with Google's existing products?

3. Who are the ultimate users of this product? How will you convince Google that these users need your product?

4. What materials will you need to create to explain and promote your product idea?

Quiz

1 To which company does Google belong?

2 Who founded Google?

3 When did the Oxford English Dictionary add "google" to its dictionary?

4 What is the name of Google's email service?

5 Where is Google's international headquarters located?

6 What does the word "googol" mean?

7 What percentage of Google's earnings come from advertising?

8 When was Google Home released?

9 What Google organization works with non-profits?

10 What percentage of internet searches begin with Google Search?

Answers

1. Alphabet Inc. **2.** Larry Page and Sergey Brin **3.** 2006 **4.** Gmail **5.** Mountain View, California **6.** An unfathomable number **7.** More than 85 percent **8.** 2016 **9.** Google.org **10.** Close to 80 percent

Key Words

acquisitions: the purchases of other companies

apps: software programs used on computers and mobile devices

assets: all of the property owned by a company or person

autonomous: operating independently

board of directors: a group of people who manage or oversee the direction of a company

brand: corporate identity

conglomerates: companies made up of several divisions

digital streaming: sending video or audio feed over the internet for immediate play

digitizing: converting to digital form for use on computers

diversified: enlarged or varied a company's range of products

hardware: the physical parts of electronic devices or computers

incorporate: to form into a legal corporation

investor: a person who commits money to a project in order to gain a financial return

liabilities: a company's debts and business costs, including wages

logo: a symbol or design used to identify a specific company

machine learning: the application of AI that allows computers to learn without programming

malware: software designed to interfere with how a computer is supposed to operate

market capitalization: the value of a company's outstanding shares

monopoly: the exclusive control by one company of a service or product

non-profit organizations: groups that conduct business for the benefit of the general public without a profit motive

parent company: a large business that has control over smaller businesses

philanthropy: making life better for other people

profitable: having money left after business costs are subtracted from sales

revenue: the amount of money a company receives for goods or services sold over a particular amount of time

slogan: a distinctive phrase used to identify a specific company

software: the programs that run a computer system

venture capital: money invested in risky new companies

Index

LIGHTBOX

SUPPLEMENTARY RESOURCES

Click on the plus icon found in the bottom left corner of each spread to open additional teacher resources.

- Download and print the book's quizzes and activities
- Access curriculum correlations
- Explore additional web applications that enhance the Lightbox experience

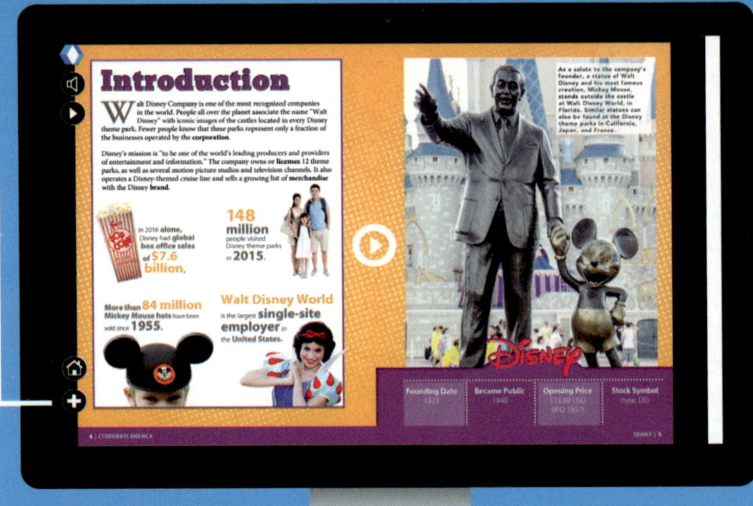

LIGHTBOX DIGITAL TITLES

Packed full of integrated media

VIDEOS

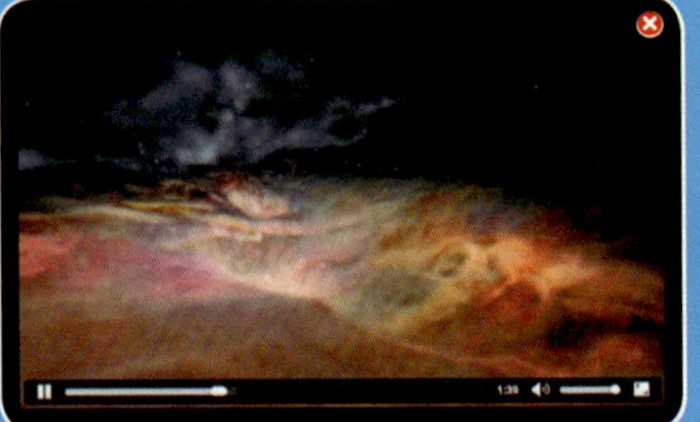

INTERACTIVE MAPS

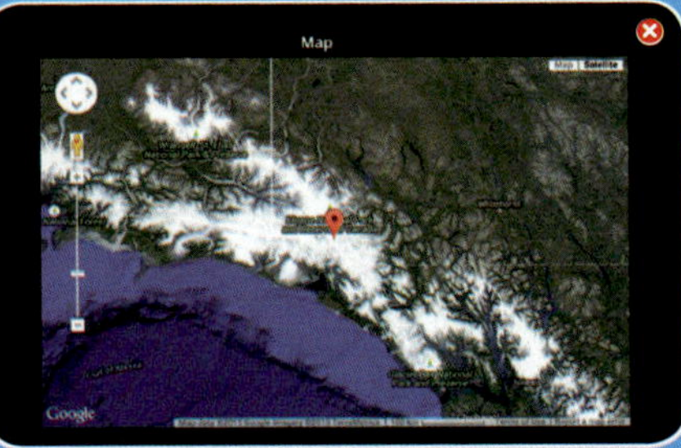

WEBLINKS

SLIDESHOWS

QUIZZES

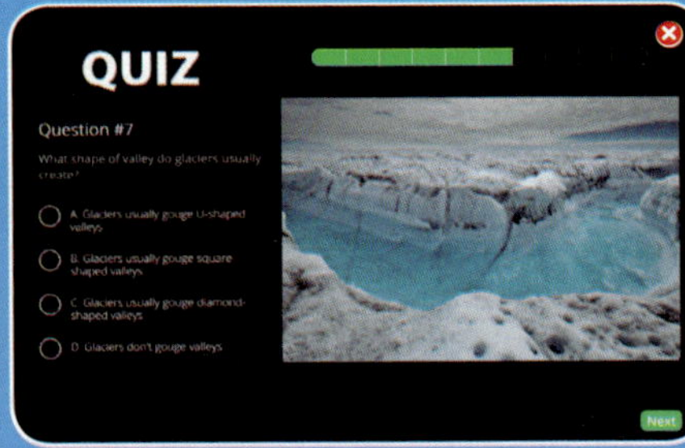

OPTIMIZED FOR

- ✓ TABLETS
- ✓ WHITEBOARDS
- ✓ COMPUTERS
- ✓ AND MUCH MORE!

Published by Smartbook Media Inc.
350 5th Avenue, 59th Floor New York, NY 10118
Website: www.openlightbox.com

Editor: Heather Kissock
Designer: Nick Newton

Library of Congress Cataloging-in-Publication Data
Names: Gregory, Joy, author.
Title: Google Alphabet / Joy Gregory.
Description: New York, NY : Smartbook Media Inc., [2019] | Series: CorporateAmerica | Includes index.
Identifiers: LCCN 2017048288 (print) | LCCN 2017049833 (ebook) | ISBN 9781510534995 (Multi-User Ebook) | ISBN 9781510534988 (hardcover : alk.paper)
Subjects: LCSH: Google (Firm)--Juvenile literature. | Alphabet Inc.--Juvenileliterature. | Internet industry--United States--Juvenile literature.
Classification: LCC HD9696.8.U64 (ebook) | LCC HD9696.8.U64 G665275 2019 (print) | DDC 338.7/610040973--dc23
LC record available at https://lccn.loc.gov/2017048288

Printed in Brainerd, Minnesota, United States
1 2 3 4 5 6 7 8 9 0 21 20 19 18 17

122017
151217

Photo Credits
Every reasonable effort has been made to trace ownership and to obtain permission to reprint copyright material. The publisher would be pleased to have any errors or omissions brought to its attention so that they may be corrected in subsequent printings. The publisher acknowledges Alamy, Getty Images, Newscom, iStock, and Shutterstock as its primary image suppliers for this title.